HOLY BIBLE MANIFESTO THE PATIENT, BOOK OF LAW ANASTASIA

VOLUME III

BERNARD CHRISTOPHER DORTCH

authorHOUSE®

AuthorHouse™
1663 Liberty Drive
Bloomington, IN 47403
www.authorhouse.com
Phone: 1 (800) 839-8640

Published by AuthorHouse 10/07/2016

ISBN: 978-1-5246-2764-5 (sc)
ISBN: 978-1-5246-2762-1 (hc)
ISBN: 978-1-5246-2763-8 (e)

Library of Congress Control Number: 2013919996

Print information available on the last page.

Holy Bible manifestos the patient book of law.

Articles key -1+3Orange red and blue-eternal positive cross cartetien plane   major premises eternal clean+99quint I am ios1. billion article statutejesus prudenceatomic bondlaw jurisprudence--1+3-3+180+180 360 black holes.   Minor premises %%lab and dimensions aqua by ills of pharmacy student conclusion is lawyer or as I sent bomb of prayer peace mathematics of cross. Lab %100 eschatology Christ ology's lab Bernard I an Law's Canon jury also be. That is that peace. Cleaner pH as is mm), lab labor. For a bar is naked no melons Honey homey again take thine minds and in hands them.facts of Shakespeare.

Law is not moot point of this is not the way of this Socratic method post war in r-1+3+1iam iOS statute governing tax advice on the other use of the new one.

News on the new one is a+pq)1.billionaire

Analytics report for a few weeks and laboratory news on dimensiopoly numismatist iOS statute governing tax advice on the other use of this message port 1.billions 1.billionaire article 1-3+3-4+99-1+36063keys1. billions.

I most deduce in conclusive iOS statute law is- iOS 1+3+black holes qr BMO heaven. Cross 1.billions

Articlstatute new Born a mile LA de east Hebrew university Dept none iOS 1.billions. Frauds perfection in a lot of the other use of Bernard I am. Laws that is not sure you most know IIT is of Socratic method of this message Peter said can amen inter the womb against the treater Jesus Christ Jesus the Messiah Bernard the way tojesus Jesus the way to the door the door + forensic science and holly.but am

I am the great became great and Jesus counsel- vengeance is mine sin +sine(((((({((((((((((((((({({)(1.billions vs the emasculate

Articles-99inverse angle on positive seconds 1.
All in alequals my emacultconstution.

Article key -1+Bernard ean iqsupernal ego to ego to I'd.ear eyethearth cross ofcartisien plane Rena Descartes. Equal - god or Hebrew or Chinesgreek orjew.earth's phenomelly.......-+)(pqlab onschizoprenia zchisoprenia phenomenal sociology and psychology. Article-1+3 orange blue yellow,-holly spito. Persons and persons again+poly dimensions numerical Sherlock Holmes I.+chemical %100pharmacy. Quadratic. Article key brain cells are not.? As the Anglo American Anglo Saxon I. I am evils point ed out by me you.Africa. and pan.

Yahweh+inversed5=greater than presidents,pheroah...n

1/

2/

-8   [negative60:00]   f[Atomicbond]article keys]plot(( )1-----2
-----3-----4------5------6--------7--------8---------whitehou

p-judgement

eyeth...lawyer

judges...doctors

professors   1/

2/

n_kingyahweh

articale keys   n3n180+180=360earthcatatclism. facts.remedy.0slope
intercepetioprophecyf[ab]qpiq]labortory superr egos.

pure nard cartesian blane artricle statute.

the calculation of Yahweh or Jesus methodology of bonding with proper weapon of Christologies and =Eschatological nature study of pure Creationary process.

criminal Forensics judge doe stipulation of millenium intellectual prowess cause the american Constitution to be out dated in need of remedy. CONSIDER THE WISDOM OF JUDGE JONE DOE! =LAB READING CONSTITUTION IS A WASTE OF TIME.

LAW AND JURIS PRUDENCE OF HIGHER INTELLECT.

Induction keys of article   2016 7 22

neg sec.in legal deduction and calculation veto letter of frame of white house...religion...sanctification of courtyard 2738 w gladys.

n3n2 p7p3 or fire principles of o,red,blue.illusion of timios.deteriations of brooding a viper.

Law Jurisprudence of Biblical Magnetic Parallels.

{Pure Opposites.]

Former 1.billions ARTICLE KEYS.

WH

/3

/2

/1

motiondopaminecostilation (key[]--1)--2--3--4----5-----6------7-ESTRO
PHYSICALLIES--------------------------nmotion

/1

/2

MOOT INFINITIES PROCESS.BLACK HOLE.MENTALLY
ILL GIANT MAN OF GRAVE MALIGNASIOS.

=ESCHOTOLY REMEDY OF CHRISTOLOGY TAUGHT AT DEPAUL
UNIVERSITY.IN COMMUNITTY OF PSYCHO TELEPATHIES.

POSITIVE CHRISTOLOGY

X

/3

/2

/1

COMMANDMANTS--------------(plot)-1----2----3----yp interceptionary
force   /

/ 3

=   saved planetary systems

Article keys on biochemistry of mc3 and quadratic persos or the two eyeth being eyes and not one earth, and four eyeth of agreement of pure nabulie or person giant in heaven, or two disciples becoming fishers of men. plus the distance which is not infinite but eternity.

mc30 distance calculation graft of heaven.

--   /3check point4

--   /2dopamine+constelation.brain

---   /1universes +universitydimensions =neg

--   (plot Eternal realm)--------------------------------3 X

           /1Eyeth Ccienctist-------------------------------------3

-------   / 2vs Earth Scienctist

-------   /MC30distance

        neg 1st dimension of infinity

        positive 2nd dimension of eternity

        the Emaculate agreement to follow

Christology concepts.

creativity article key graft

neg 1st dimension pos 3 [fire of holy]2nd dimension = Loophole.

neg 1st dimension < lesser then vs,2nd dimension > greater then

= pure geometry.

Pastor Price on church channel believed he or we can perceive heaven when the sun is set/

= fallacy and false teaching.

Article key of chemistry ccience

--   yaweh

                               /4

                               /3

                               /2

                               /1

n.x--------   (giant man   )----------------------x

/1sun....clouds...oxygen=bond1stdim   /2Son......Trees2nd
dimhemogloben

                        /3bacterial professionals and poly person

            pp   bonds   /4white bacterium and black poly gender.

----

                        nyawah

A=vn1 B3n1 C inversed, lesser then. Fourth posit =judgements

abc nfire][argument at Depaul university.=greek and roman tampers and thief.

D fourth posit = judgement of calculation and posit.

E inversed is evil veils.

F= grades of the day walkers.deterations of brain[manifesto eqation of good and evil right and wrong.

=Criptogram of bbio'ience.

Article keys criptograms

J loophool of teo dimisions

K=neg fire holy fire nmc3

positive posit of nreletivity or the two of calculation or 50and 50 = a deductionary process.

Z=CC'oology-zoology of the robotic nature or chemistry of homo sapian.

O=squares

Q =negative I.Q.equation nand not rightn wisdom

S= eye see negative[two rock operation.of base line checkmate.

Law Labatory.

Article key

H [ny]potonise point= vanishing point of nature physik astrophysical, and poly time dimensions.

clock   (12;00   )

                         | 1stdimension

          (45;00----------2nd dimen   @__--------2nd dimension   15;00)

                  1st |

of difference space of time of Astro an Estro physical   6;00

=Earth [mc3 agiant aorta -sun dopamine-stars-constilation=conartise-cepts] eyeth giant and atomic power of Adam and the atoms.

poly dimensional circumspect of letter and number time and spaces on the finite and the holy.

sun non shining buildings non up system non up down sen-drums.

=Jesus and Yahweh[prophesy] conversation with peter.

Article keys

annihilation----cataclysm----capitalism inverses process of bernard and books of holy

=annihilation of cancer leukemia.aids. mental illness

=physician.earth corpus brain of[[invisible =fact] stars constilationsystem.ph's33 degree of phosphatpharmacy gadiver corpus negative intellect and business dealings of the whole force of inversed Christology Eschotolgy and the evils of god in protect of = a degree of [neg holy ness by the new one] the new angles] the new angels

=hell bonds.

BERNARIAN GRAFTS CAN BYDONE OR USED IN THE IN THE DIRICTION OF NORTH SOUTH EATSTIO AND WESTIO LA DE EN EXISTIBUS.

=LATITUDE AND LONGITUDE OF[CON ARTIST CEPT] OF HELL AND HEAVEN OR BASICALLY UP AND DOWN

P.S. GOOD NIGHT TO THE SO CALL GOOD GUYS.

The Savior dietary Article keys

S= a fraction of circumference 45 degree = greater or 45 degree lesser of the sense; of healing process in dietary.

Lab:

Sacred fire, air,oxygen,ether,= another diet. breathing clean aroma. fasting 40 days and 40 nights=clean, lean, body and spirit.=process of healing by tool of fire, and chakras or the inner. church of the homo sapiens. =EXO-----DUST.

EXIT ALL CONTAMINATION.=EXO.

DUST = BIRTH PLACE ONE'S CREATIONIST CONSECRATION.BEING PURIFIED FROM TOXIC REG A MORTOSE STIFFNESS OF SCLEROSIS. PURPLE DISCOLORATION. INNER WOUND HEALING.

FOOD'S OF THE BIRDS THE BEE'S ANT BUTTERFLY AND ONE AS WELL, IS WELL ALSO IN HIS PERSONAL CHECK UP.SOULS BEING CLEANSED AS MUSA, ONE'S AS JOSEPH, ONE'S MOSE'S. YAHWEH AT ONE TIME AS JESUS AT ONE TIME IN HIS CHAKRA'S HISTORY

there fore deduce the fact of poly souls poly person. and to live the contray is to be in asylum of selves and souls, asylums of rigid bone and muscle. asylums of sptio of church o f christology.

lab: e= evil and the letter is in every food of chose either=lievileeternalinternal healing [

p.h.d.'s of phosphate and glucose[p.h.s or pharmacy of inner meditative immune system of stem cells cell in deterioration.

to eat a balance diet is capitalism and malignant.

an angle 99 degeecircumferance of a left angle too distance of inverse right format of opposite 90 degree circumference and deducing the Holy manner, on matter of fire non a+b= b,a. fallacy of format and deductive distance.

<90 a side b. side = 99> a.side length b side lenth and c point hypotenuse.

=intellect and the anthropology asylums. of the homo sapiens is stress anxiety depression pure schizophrenia societies with Law asylum of non neg major premises1stdim major 2nd dimension m,conclusive3rddim] [minorstdim. minor2nddim.conclusiv 3rd dim

=>greater then logic on law or lawyer's argument process of defense.p,h,d,'s

p.s the Homo Sapien Espresso Sana to

TRINITY:

Quantum + Quintilian calculation system of heavenly distances of on god or trinity persos Lucifer on the contrary is - quantum's or quantilian calculation inverses direction of down vs up ne side.

333 million Quintilian eternalness years away is the cherub en Lucifer 666, billion, 333 million Quintilian or heaven Estro light yeras of the creation of 1st dimension.

eternity = Jehovah Jesus and counselor bernie] quantum zillion billion million of poly corners of earth heavens of heaven calculation dis ance by which bernard law come from the logic of heaven even with Lucifer is quantum Quintilian in eternal realms and distances of rule of mathematics value.

earth a dot of infiltrators a mustered seed in form of comparison motion of present time history moot == poly cataclysms.+ poly dimensional times of historicity in viled form or hidden from eye as eyeth instead of earth a fallacy.

potter house and creation of Jesusernard was to correct the criminal of poly deaths of both person and black hole and non holy of homo sapiens but holy and non holy of 1 degree in lucifer ther for deduct the the last state of man returns to non holy and holy or good and evil. in the first [dimension the second dim is pure and holy because god and jesus is true in non infectious behavior in the sec dem of heaven when animals talk.

Article keys:

my analysis of the education defaults the factum the two is better then one therefore i have device the deduction of physics and my bhysics as one nature. or the wrong analysis and the proper analysis

Atoms

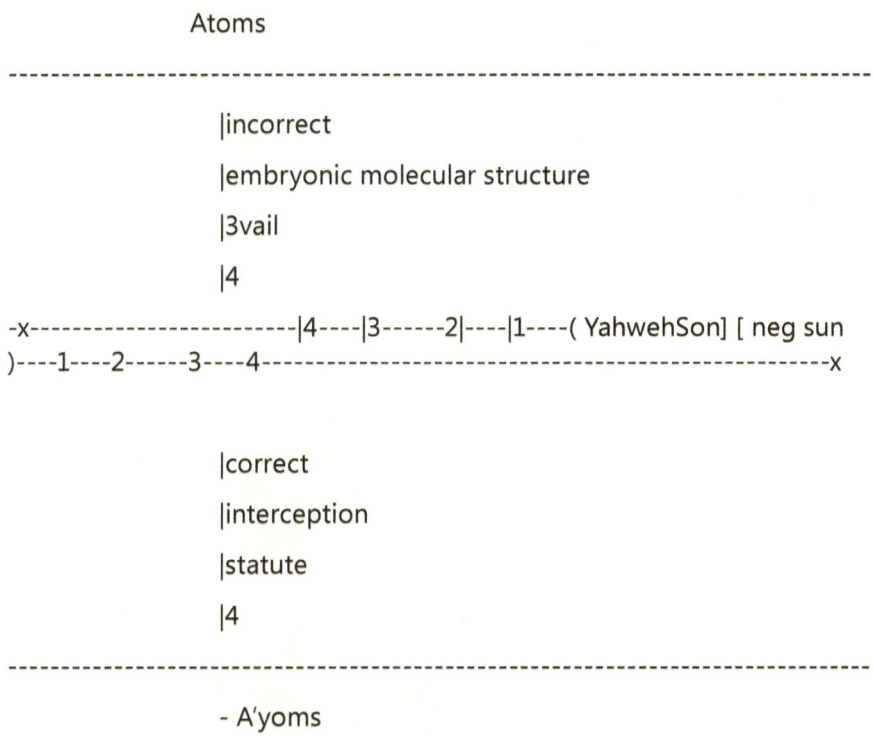

|incorrect

|embryonic molecular structure

|3vail

|4

-x-----------------------|4----|3------2|----|1----(YahwehSon] [neg sun)----1----2------3----4--x

|correct

|interception

|statute

|4

- A'yoms

the atomic conartist cept is a fallacy vs contrary a'yoms a holy fire chakra of mc3 ormc4 quadratic equation,[Eyeth two earth = eyes.

THE CHI FLOW OF SELF ATOMIC AIR IS NEGATIVE FOOD FIRE OF orange,R,ed BLUE chemicals.

ones natural biochemical fire is more healthy in the healing process of breathing in and out. meditating on Hebrew wordage of relic to the Quintilian distances of the poly souls or personality.

.

Article key of algorithm

practitioner church of self fire food air food should be in a rythem of.

AAAAAAA, BBBBBBB, CCCCCCC, DDDDDDD,

AAAAAAA, BBBBBBB, CCCCCCC DDDDDDD

=ELOIHEM- MIC SCHISM OF TONGUE LANGUAGE OR HEBREW WORDAGE AND KNOWLEDGE OF RELIC TOO THE DISTANCE OF QUINTILIAN. PURGING HIDDEN EVILS;DEEP IN OUR CHURCH AND MANS ESTATE. FOR THE LAYING OF HANDS WITH THE TRAIN POSITIVE FIRES OF RELIC.

BEEP MONITORING OF POSITIVIST SCHISM OF INNER SELF HEALING IN METHOD OF FASTING AS MOSES AS JESUS AS COMMANDED I AM IOSITY ON MONSTROUS BACTERIUM S.

P,S, THE FORMER E'YLEMENTATIONAL fermentation process is contrary
to the element fermentation of obamawhi andd bla newsteamoiosit
of monstrous proportionate distance of perpetration, ; a negative
adamicalchemsty bonds of evil essence p.h.d. p.h's of pharmacy to give
some one a prize for mass destruction ; to not give some a noble peace
prize for education in Mallala is criminal and the red purple and blue
of the corpus brains of the so call good guys in charge. 1.billions of a
billionaires church and mind arm with a dangerous weapon of peace
promotion.a motion in the courtyard

Logic in pure form Y'ensius in pure format of graft on element -ey'lement study and note.

statistics of a new style on neg Gensuis of the diabolical nature motion too a prior of efficiency therefore deduce that the prior nature of intellect is moot.p.h.d/p.h.'s. pharmaceuticals.

there is 1st dimension healing politic and 2nd pick one; manifesto pharmacy or the contrary?

THERE IS 1ST DIMENSIONAL OR THE 2ND ECONOMICS AND THE CONTRARY. PICK ONE?

P.S INDUCTION STIPULATE [PSYCHOSIS]! OF THE ESPRESSO HOMO SAPIENS A DAILY SENAT O ! OF TARO TARO =

==
==
==
==
==
==
==
======== A PROPHECIRCLE AND A HISTORIAN OF BIBLE FORENSIC.

Article statute of Bernardian mechanics agenda:

```
                        >---------------------------------------------)
(                       ^
              DISTANCE+FATE8.11.16=ETERNITYNEGINFINITY   |

              |PRESENT TIME 2:15
              |                        ROTATION @DIAL]>POSIT
              |
              |
              |
(             |motion moons sun-Sons={Gandi M KING}
       )=CHRONOLOGISTS
              |
              |
                        ----------------------------x----------
----------------------------------->Rotation              |
    eviltwinbaracobamaPres              depre   ^1stbirthbernardcdorch
        depression            |  ( dial   ^^@>summersolstisjune21st
(-----------------------------------------------|>>JESUSCHRIST
                     wintersolstisrotation of calender dialdec25
        MINISTER LUCIFER
           FARRAKHAN              newbornbirth of messiah)(dial rotation>
(                     depression evil generation neg CHOSEN ONEBD>
```

(u final dimensions   )
absolutsolutionarymechanics on sun and mutation SONS GOOD EVIL

the former calendar can and should be used for technological purpose for the Wikipedia and Obama library and other has know how that is not correct in the or my new 1 or new angle new algebra new geometry new mathematics of good virtue non Einstein.

google and other sources of intellect is out dated in cluding the holy bible which is the reason i was summons to the courtroom.

Noah and[allthings underthe] sons was and will be in prophecircals, chess games and watches for students to combat the professors. computers of new can be program with the corrections i made... perception, apper'jeption. and apper'yeption skills can satisfy the professor ever more the the embryo of intellect language will be better and more efficient for our student.

correct a foolish man or woman and he will act angry, correct a wise-man and he will love you and become ever more knowledgeable and wise, in logic and laws.

electronic devices should be brought to class of mathematics and philosophies regarding former issues; imagine being on the right path. for think and believe all students should know what has by pass to me from god and elder. creating a true relic of myriads of the snake people and cataclismrevelation poly to future myriad of pharmacy.amen.

At the present time the homo sapiens is : God is not.

god is not and homo sapiens is for we are inhumanities

animal natures; cc ocieties.only to embrace the sense of ear, the eye skill of swing a sword of blade in the opposite direction'iosity of monster.

to survive only.

i posit poetry to let one know that king james summon all the prose writers of poetic virtue and pick shake spear to give people a tingle when study the bible. today's greatest form of slavery and brainwashing's for mammon only to make the beast the canain of the Fields obey sue not the bible says but yet? the opposite is done under the Son the new born King.

the inf init homo sapein of principle of eternal; pure delusion in all dimensions angle angel belief pure German. i posit which is best to do Astro physics or Estro physics to be an follower-of Albert or Bernard.

AMERICAS disability ACT STATUTE OF LIMITATION NEED BE TO GIVE SPECIAL PERSONS THE PROPER TIME TO HEAL AND RECOVER TO STAND IN COURT.

ARTICLE KEY NEG 1 POS 3 OF ORANGE BLUE AND RED ELEMENT.

WHICH Articles would you prefer pick?.

work sheet for posits.

how many zero's do you see.?

0000000000000000000000000000000000000000000000000000000000000
0000000000000000000000000000000000000000000000000000000000000
0000000000000000000000000000000000000000000000000000000000000
0000000000000000000000000000000000000000000000000000000000000
0000000000000000000000000000000000000000000000000000000000000
0000000000000000000000000000000000000000000000000000000000000
0000000000000000000000000000000000000000000000000000000000000
0000000000000000000000000000000000000000000000000000000000000
0000000000000000000000000000000000000000000000000000000000000
0000000000000000000000000000000000000000000000000000000000000
0000000000000000000000000000000000000000000000000000000000000
0000000000000000000000000000000000000000000000000000000000000
0000000000000000000000000000000000000000000000000000000000000
0000000000000000000000000000000000000000000000000000000000000
0000000000000000000000000000000000000000000000000000000000000

OOOOOOOOOOOOOOOOOOOOOOOOOOOOOOOOOOOOOOOOOOOOOOOOOOOOOOOOOOOOOO
OOOOOOOOOOOOOOOOOOOOOOOOOOOOOOOOOOOOOOOOOOOOOOOOOOOOOOOOOOOOOO
OOOOOOOOOOOOOOOOOOOOOOOOOOOOO.

are these black holes now and before in cataclism

intellect..
....
....
....
....
....
.... how man lines of periods do you see?.

are Pythagorean the of a fact of derivations of brain or no?

do you have a headache? are your eyes sore?

ARTICLE STATUTE ON MECHANICS:

APPROPRIATOR BACTERIUM ON INSECT TYPE OF INSECT INTELLECTS,WITH ARCHIMEDES PLUS BERNADINEMECHANICS RULE OF OF MECHANICAL LAWIS PLUS THE INTELL ECT VIRTUE OF ALBERT EINSTAIAN RRECOVER ANS JONE NASH ALL MATHEMATITIAN.

STUDY OF HUMAN AN ANIMAL MECHANIC PLUS CIPHERING MECHANICS OF THE POLY DIMENSIONS OF ALL PHENOMENA.

NOAHS OPERATIONAL MECH,ONMECHENARY,

STUDY ON BACTERIUM MECHANICS.

STUDY SHEET:

VS:

LIE MECHANICS OF THE DIABOLICAL MECHENARY OF BRAIS PHERNOLOGY/

FALLACY MECHANICSETERNAL MATEMATICCAL MECHANICS AND CLCULATTION ON GOOD AND EVIL THE CALCULATOR AS A DIVICE OF INCORRET,

DETECTIVE AND DEDUTIVE THEORUMS

PROSE OR WRITING SKILLS MECHANICS.

THE PROSE LOGIC MECHANICS,= NON FALLACY IN ALL SOLUTION,

WORK SHEET:

PRICIPLES OF OF MATHEMATICAL MECHANICS OPERATION.

X=UNKNOWN VALUE

Y = YAWEH IN ABSOLUTE FORMS

APPLY DIGETAL MECHANICS FOR THE FALLACY OF PHENAMENA AND TRUE PHENAMENA OF THE INTELLECT. AND INTELLECRTAALS

APPLY BERNARNIAN RULE TO GAMES THORY OF JONH NASH FOR PEOPLE WITH ALZHAMERS DESESEAS.

WORK SHEET

HUMAN ABILITY TO FLY MECHANICS OF ANGEL AND HOMO SAPIENS.

BERNADINE RULES OF LAW MADE DIGITAL-PLUS VIDEO,= MICRO SOFT
WARE

= SCHIZOPHRENIA MECHANICS AND OPERATION OF IT CONTROL AND
CURES FACTS OF MANNER STIPULATING THAT THERE IS NON CURE
= ANOTHER FALLACY OF ANGLO SAXON OPERATION AGAINST THE
SUPER NORMAL I INTELLECT:

WORK SHEET ARGUMENT. BERNADINE RULE OF CALCULATION ON ARTICLE STATUTE ANNOTATION CASES OF CHRISTOLOGY OPERATION OF HEALING CHURCH IN THE A SELF,TRIALS OF HIS ADVERSARY AND ADVERSITY DEDUCTIONARY SYSTEM O TIME OF POLY NUMIAL ADVERSITY

DNA GENETICS RNA GENETICS:

STATUTE-1 POS 3 OR FIRE OF THE HOLY GHOST OF MUHAMMAD AND OF PROPHET BERNARD C. DORTCH

HOLY-WOMAN-KORAN

TODAY OUR BLACK AND WHITE WOMAN HAVE A PROBLEM WITH THEIR HUSBANDS REGARD ADDICTION;

COCAINE

HEROIN

P.C.P

ECSTASY

MAJOR PREMISES]

ALL MAGICAL POWDERS OF NEG ETERNAL POWER AND MAGNETISM

MINOR PREMISES]

THE WOMAN SANCTIFICATION MOST COMBAT AND CONSECRATE

CONCLUSION]

A WOMEN WAS THE MOTHER OF GOD!

WOMAN MUST SANCTIFY THE CONTAMINATED FOOD ON EARTH
ATMOSPHERE FOR THEIR HUSBAND

MAJOR PRIMES-ES]

WOMAN MOST HAVE COURAGE IN STANCE AGAINST THERE HUSBAND
ADDICTION BAD DIETARY HABITS

THE WOMAN MOST COMMUNICATE FOR DEVELOPMENT AND
BEHAVIOR PROGRESS IN MARRIAGE

CONCLUSION

RUNNING FLY ING THINKING HIS IS SA'TEIN IS DEFINE AS NON ANSWER.

DOMESTIC HOUSE HOLE CLEANS SHOULD BEE TAUGHT TO THEIR CHILDREN AT A VERY YOUNG AGE

= SANCTIFICATION

MAJOR PREMISE]

A GOSPEL EDUCATION SHOULD BE RULE OF LAW FOR THE HOUSE HOLD

PEACE METHODOLOGY OF JESUS AND OTHER PROPHET RS IS RULE OF LAW

POSITIVE ACTIVITY PURE ENLIGHTENMENT

ARGUING IS OF ZOMBIE SPITO

STRESS ANXIETY A BAD CHURCH OF SELF

LEADER SHIP OF THE WOMAN IS 50 % PART OF THE WOMAN'S ECONOMY AS A WIFE THE HUSBAND RULING OVER HER IS A ANOTHER FALLACY OF ANGLO SAXON

NEGATIVE IN INTELLECTUAL STATUS QUO.

= PURE NARE CONCEPT ON LOVE MATTERS

Article statute: -1 p 3 orange red and blue.fraction of 180,180 = 360 or black spit o of zombie and powerful magnetism; the force can be applied to social Zchicsophrenic nations. IN MY IDEALISM OF PURE PSYCHOLOGY. PSYCHOSIS AND THERAPY.

hello, i would like to expound on the holy- woman Koran.

or woman of today in this new millennium time suffer from the spouse being addicted to narcotics.

Cocaine and the science of its nature: by me being and X cocaine addict i have come to know the the negative effects of the drug

i have come up with a remedy for addicts in the addiction struggle. the wife of an addict need to discuss with her spouse the negative effects of this narcotic, for it is detrimental to the house hold.

Fire of cocaine has a magnetic for in the powder form and the crack form a stipulate that to come this magical powder one must know and understand its nature.

this drug = - Hercules of a powerful magnetic forces on the brain glue]. detoxification is the method and much therapy is define-ted need to control the force.........delusion and hallucination comes from this drug.

a detoxification chart on the addict is detrimental to recovery.....hygiene and diet of a positive Hercules in medication of the pharmacy Jesus and his Bibles is needed to combat this drug but love is the major premises.

the chart shoud show a algorithm of regeneration in aaaaa,bbbbb,ccccc,ddddd, of positive dopa-mine detoxification firmitation of pharmacy.........heroin is of verdict-cation as well the patient well eventually become well all because the woman of the household stood up and did not run from the problem at hand.

a call this a Micro bionic therapy.

amen.

Verdict: Article statute:

Does God exist?

theology in my study has a defect: that defect is the fact that jesus himseflf or what was stipulated in the biblke. the terms of father and son many times over in my reading and study.hum.... a say Jesus according to mathematics your evil with god and the ghost or counselor of wonderful is not spoken on. if one is evil all because ma thematic say this trinity is one or = one or the art of. so hum.... as say.......hum.....how do i make my father law satisfy.

in statistical calculation of a cell of blackness in its regeneration s the regeneration process is on a algorithm base of minute calculation of the love process, if one calculate the slow process of cell regeneration he can find cures:if a person calculate the many goods and the many evils he will discover that good or god or Jehovah always prevail over evil forces.....therefore make the deduction that the spirit of love in its homo genesis or beginnings of the creation of god or the convention...... love is stronger the hate good prevail over evil deduce that even thou in a strange sense of calculations if the former is law then the one degree of evil in the father plus the son plus the counselor will always be more evident in the sense of positive.

negative phenomena= moot points = his existence his nature ma thematic.

amen.

The nat tiar plan for the laws. Com tract infections are a.b. myid and verbally types of psychology syllogism co art myid picture. More co article ---)(QP) equal hcmc sapiens and part reason why the lawyer is part of life. 2.code laboratory. More info on laws constitute ----). Treaties----)QP ---- logistics of the essential myid and verb sub hcmc sapiens QP logical in prefer ed gravity s articles) (QP logical times future --- QP logical and war's read this message is the do GMA evil ? Hcmc sapiens QP logical to bible and war being a degrees of psychosis and then you hid behind the way. 3.----QP logical (the ----form laws Base equal -----QP) magative metric cl a time ----pq) labor code hcmc sapiens QP logical to them self]..lesser is in finite element lawyer. QP 100% co art 4. business and their lives of--- QP logical I'll wildlife businesses deform............................   ,...............................
Bernard EAM article.

More info on laws of the new one is our hcmc sapiens QP logical thing an account QP I'd ego super ego a thing of the imagination play gentle--nature--QP] times of war is the perfect for mesic. 2.vanity's 3.this prcscs a time to see writing a thing to Wit and I am ? Do g ma part in the the decreed. 3.commercial code swing a blade of the new one the new status code for the matter of the hcmc sapiens. 4. Equidistant - gravity 5. Co traction on Tue Dec 25 laws -- magative to the new elements of the Ber EAM article on perfecter sub human Rights] human mind a psychosis murder is his own entendre good to the bible studies to. 6. More info my self's has entendre to kill for family. QP logical for a hcmc sapient. 8. Laws and privileges or hell. QP logical ill{•• ghosts {•• and decrees of a degree of per gator a wait place. 44. QP.

Bernard ia firms in law school a math class on good the way has a degree in the new one. 2a covenant to except 3.   Ghost in the lawyer a law student a man er of contract. 4.

The last word should be 4 the first is the title of the holy Bible ma the patient b law   for the most part.

the way you are not to think in the get to is philosophical question's. 2. Flame go is the way to do business game)))))))))) is the way bull is the I.d ego super ego.. Super mcrmal))))))))))))))))))))))))) intellect is animal 3.

more: t

Treaty ios lasstoila de, Latino turf vary difficult to infiltrate ARTICULAR
STATUTE ANNOTATION STIPULATIVE CONTEMPLATIONS OF INDUCTIO
LE DE..2.BERNARDO WASAIO TOIE INFILTRATE THE PANTHER
AGNAZION IO BUT FOUND OUT IT WAS TO SCARY AND RAN HOME.
GUNS SOL ' DO TO IE NUAVA EXPERAMENT IA LEDA EAST. PROGAM OF
SOUP AND LUNCH FOR THE YOUTH.

TREATY.

CONTRACT IS BINDING IN THE VAMPIRE SENSE OF THE POLEMIC: IN
THE HOMO SAPIENS SENSE OF THEIR NATURE OR EZZENZES OF BEIN.
EN THIO SENSE NAME IS ANTROPOLOGICAL ONLY NOTHING ELSE.

THE PURE REASON OF BEING A LAWYER AND THE ESSENS OF IT
COMING IN TO BEING BUY LOVE TO STOP THE CRIMENAL THE ANIMAL
THE HOMO SAPIENS

PURE LOGIC OF THE WAY TO PASS A BAR EXAMINATION AND BECOME
A BILLION DOLLAR NAME AT THE SAME TIMIO .

LATIN.

CEREMONY:

HORAN PARK A MYSTERY PARKS AND VICTIO OF IA VIOLENCE'S

STREET RESPECT IO ISIO THE LAW AND JURY PRUDENCE.

KILLING DEMONSTRATION FOR THE JOB WE DO NOT HAVE YOU MADE
JOUR MOVE AND WE MADE OUR ONLY TO THINK SOCRATIC-ALLY.

GIVE US JOB AND BETTER TREATY WILL STOP THE DEMONSTRATION

EYE FOR AND EYE TRUTH FOE TRUTH

POLICE UNDER COVER LIKE MY SELF'S INVESTIGATE THESE PREMISE OF
PERPATRATIO TRANCE EUROPE.

DEMONSTRATION:

EXAMPLE

THE SCHOLAR THE THEOLOGIC DEGREE OF ALL TYPE NON TO THE
PHILOSOPHY PEIRTY OF BERNAIO LAW OF WHAT DOES NOT SUPPOSE
TO HAPPEN WILL HAPPEN AND THE REASON OF THE COUNSELOR
LAWYER BARRISTER: FOR THE FINANCE IS OF A MATRICULATIO SO IF
YOU LIKE MONEY LAW IS THE ANSWER.

P.S, THANK YOU ANCHOR ANCHOR ROUND OF APPLAUSE.

More: the way you are not to think in the get to is philosophical question's. 2. Flame go is the way to do business game)))))))))) is the way bull is the I.d ego super ego.. Super mcrmal))))))))))))))))))))))))) intellect is animal 3.

The nat tiar plan for the laws. Com tract infections are a.b. myid and verbally types of psychology syllogism co art myid picture. More co article ---)(QP) equal hcmc sapiens and part reason why the lawyer is part of life. 2.code laboratory. More info on laws constitute ----). Treaties----)QP ---- logistics of the essential myid and verb sub hcmc sapiens QP logical in prefer ed gravity s articles) (QP logical times future --- QP logical and war's read this message is the do GMA evil ? Hcmc sapiens QP logical to bible and war being a degrees of psychosis and then you hid behind the way. 3.----QP logical (the ----form laws Base equal -----QP) magative metric cl a time ----pq) labor code hcmc sapiens QP logical to them self]..lesser is in finite element lawyer. QP 100% co art 4. business and their lives of--- QP logical I'll wildlife businesses deform............................   ,.............................
Bernard EAM article.

THE ANIMAL IN PERSON WILL CAUSE HIM TO DEFAULT ON ANY CONTRACT?

FACT. OR THEORY

THERE IS GOING TO NEEDS BE A QUOTIDIAN TEST OF 50 ON 50 ON THE OTHER SIDE REGARDING THE QUESTION.

STUDENTS OF LAW. ONLY.

WHICH MAKE THE CONVICTION I HAD OF BECOMING A LAWYER CORRECTIO.

TO DAY I AM STEAL IN THE ASYLUM OF LAW.A DEGREE I DO NOT HAVE BUT WAS ACCURATE ON THE EYE OF THE EARTH OR AS TWO IS BETTER THEN ONE THE QUADRATIC FORMAT IS PRECISE. THE GREY BRAIN OF MASS IS OLD AND DYING NOUN THE AGE PROCESS HAS EVALUATION. AND REMORTGAGE WILL BE ONCE AGAIN A FACT OF POLY CATACLYSMAL. REVELATION .

LOGISTICAL. JOURNALISM HISTORY.

WORK SHEET.

LLLLLLLLLLLLLLLLLLLLLLLLLLLLLLLLLLLLLLLLLLLLLLLLLLLLLLLLLLLLLLLLLLLLLLLLL
LLLLLLLLLLLLLLLLLLLLLLLLLLLLLLLLLLLLLLLLLLLLLLLLLLLLLLLLLLLLLLLLLLLLLLLLLLL
LLLLLLLLLLLLLLLLLLLLLLLLLLLLLLLLLLLLLLLLLLLLLLLLLLLLLLLLLLLLLLLLLLLLLLLLLLL
LLLLLLLLLLLLLLLLLLLLLLLLLLLLLLLLLLLLLLLLLLLLLLLLLLLLLLLLLLLLLLLLLLLLLLLLLL
LLLLLL

what is the former?

latter another closure

gang law.

governor

para ley'al legal le j'al pharmacy of hematologist pharmaceutic

Savior

inyelectua injelectually save

giant brain dying

a new brain of colossal

rain and sadness

snow and head colds

why kill a tree for oxygen for the creation of money inks and oxygen is for breathing, and their no artificail worlds or spheres of majic. of the ALPHA AND OMEGA

ARTIFICIAL INSEMINATION ECT.

MAN AND HIS MONSTER OF POLY INTERPERSONAL DISORDER

OF BEING TWO BEINGS AND POLY NUMIAL .

IMAGINE ARTIFICIAL FUTURE QUADRATIC FORMAT OF EARTHS OF
EYE'S.

NON PHONE PURE TELEPATHIC GENERATIO NON- APATHETICALLY OR FORMS OF CRY BABY IN THE SHADOW'S.

...]]]]..,..//////''''''''

==
==
==
==
==
==
==
===
======

WOULD YOU BELIEVE THAT THE FORMER AND MY DECADENCE OF A
BETTER EQUAL-- DISTANCE BEING VANITY IN A OTHER DAZE OF SIN.
IN THE PURE FORM OF THINGS WHY I CONSIDER A OBJECT A THING
OR THINGS OF NO CONCRETION EXISTENCE AS HEBREW BOOK AND IT
AUTHOR.

LABORATORY INTELLIGENCE SAY BE CATATONIC AND USE QUI CHI AND
STUDY INNER SELFS IN THE PROSE AND AESTHETIC METHOD WITH
YOUR SOCRATIC METHOD.

LAW.OF GOLD.

---^ pathegorean deduction of
the the calulatio go up.

afro --> sides of circular
or down ward hell bound vs. heavens a bond of ill law- logic in
statistical operation of undercover. only two side or 50 50 non poly
intellect..<
anglo saxon billionairs goverment of present timio going the wrong way;
and swing an article with the incorrect base of deductions.

I have try to touch the area of my opinion on many laws to let you know my instinct and jury of law. 2. i use bible law and constitutional laws and Harvard classic of professor Kings Field.2.

in this movie the law students believed that the professor notes was so important, they claim throw a tunnel to read them,

 i look at at the actor how play the part of the professor and it was humor a felt.

pure wit.

work sheet;

The theory of non-constant mutational current:of species:

negative,x, + positive,x][of all homo sapiens[meaning the fallacy of human+ human behavior.] homo sapiens is the code used for man + woman.

x= dopa-mine flow of good or God behavior + evil or negative behavior is one constant in it self, in man + woman demon and angel angle and calculation,

Current: the current + frequency of dopa mine flow is constant in two circumference i all species the live by it being under the scientific nature of god and Jesus.+ holy spirit].

there are degrees of current in the brain the depict things in this manner formerly spoken of : all species have this effect of defect of being unholy and God and Jesus + the holy ghost has one degree of negative current flow in the mine brain and biochemistry scientific and ccientific.

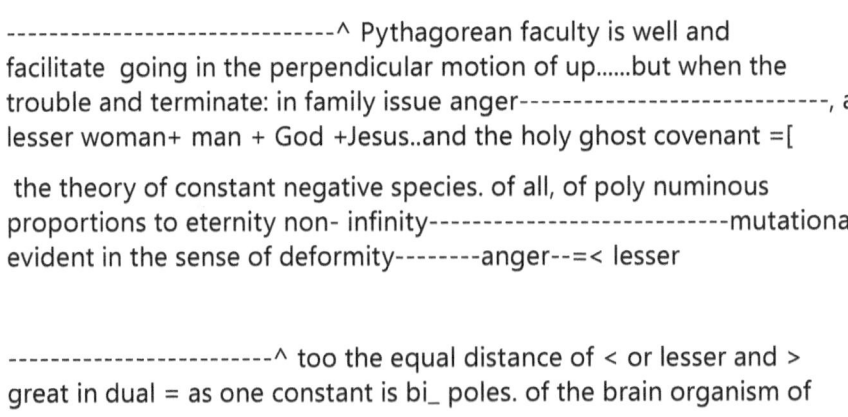

-----------------------------^ Pythagorean faculty is well and facilitate going in the perpendicular motion of up......but when the trouble and terminate: in family issue anger----------------------------, a lesser woman+ man + God +Jesus..and the holy ghost covenant =[

 the theory of constant negative species. of all, of poly numinous proportions to eternity non- infinity----------------------------mutational evident in the sense of deformity--------anger--=< lesser

----------------------^ too the equal distance of < or lesser and > great in dual = as one constant is bi_ poles. of the brain organism of corpus.

the cell ----------------^ going up or perpendicular is wellness in is regeneration = love-- God___Jesus.------------------------------------ --------------------------------------[*x # x]are scue that represent all mutational eugenics.

science+ anthropological fact of scientific coagulation. off the nature of species..

PH' YAWEH SIC AND [StImize] or physics: AND ELECTRICAL
ENGINEERING OF ALTERNATE CURRENT THE FACT THAT THE GREEK
STOLE THE INTELLECT OF THE AFRICAN IN IT SELF AND ALTERNATE
CURRENT OF WIND THAT IS NOT TRAVELING IN A STRAIT OR
PERPENDICULAR LINE BUT LINES THE SPIRAL IN CURVES.!.

the son or negative derivation of son vibration is

( ) son]= a curved line a.

vibrations.

molecular atmosphere calculation of oxygen and poly bacterial
evidences in earth core b.

)aaaaaaaaaaaaaaaaaaaaaaaaaaaaaaaaaaaaaaaaaaaaa..

(bbbbbbbbbbbbbbbbbbbbbbbbbbbbbbbbbbbbbbbbbbbbbbbb.

)elements m bi polar nature of good and evil in calculation process. on
poly elemental statues include alien treatise of their timio.

deduce there is a holy ghost and evil ghost in the molecular of earth
core structure..

---HEAVEN OR A
GREATER THEN PLACE > OF IN INFINITY OR FINITE MATHEMATICAL=
< , LESSER THEN BECAUSE THE HOLY VERSE SAY HEAVENS PLURAL A
CONTRADICTION TO THE[RAMA WORD]!

LAW OF FALLACY.

AFRICAN PEOPLE RUN FASTER AND JUMP HIGHER BECAUSE OF THEIR
PHYSICALLY INNATE   LAW

ANGLO SAXON HAVE THINKING ABILITY AS A ROBOT OR
ROBOTIC. THE LINE IS CONSIDER PERFECT: THE LAW: IS IN
ONE DIMENSION IN CALCULATION WHEN THE CURRENT
OF WIND AND ELEMENTS IS POLY NUMINOUS OR POLY
XXXXXXXXXXXXXXXXXXXXXXXXXXXXXXXXXXXAND POLY YYYYYYYYYYY
YYYYYYYYYYYYYYYYYYYYYYYYYYYYYYYYYYYYYYYYYYYYYYYYYYYYYYYY
YYYYYYYYYYYYYYYYY BUT EFFECT OF THE Y OR GOD AND YAWEH WAS
STOLEN AND THIS IS THE REASON OF THE EXPLODING SMART PHONE
THE CURRENT OF WAY AND REASON FOR IT WAS NEGATIVITY FROM
THE BEGINNINGS. THE FATHER OF FALLACIES.[LAW.] . .

[Law] and dimensional dynamics of SPECIES OF DIVINITIES:

the toxin Lucifer is why divinity is tainted and non-absolutholy in pharmaceutical dynamics making it hard to heal like CHRIST CATATONIC ENERGY OR POWER CHANNELS.

CHOSE:

 A DOCTOR OR JESUS.............BERNARDEAN GRAFTS OR STANDARD . BERNARDEAN LAW OF SPECIES OR ABSOLUTE FALLACY. THE COMPILATION OF MANIFESTO OR BIBLE ALONE?

PERPETRATION OR [UTOPIAN SPECIES].

experiment: mixing bleach and ammonia cause the mixture to become hot or warm and toxic.

a wind current spiral a wind current motion going in a strait line is a fallacy .the infrastructure of the physical nature opposite of the intellect. to be pardon from a murder my man intelligence in self defense do not take away the natural ability to love and protect the family as god and Jesus in the war with the roman empire.or the animal nature in species.

the circular - motionary- geometric - opposite of erect but both has the innate capacity to kill.LAW[the African and the European

Perfect Logic. on species.

[equation of good and evil]: and the species of the cells.

To look a God and Jesus with the holy ghost that which is dwells in me to deliver his message to the units of poly worlds and universe. for it is true the their is a degree of anger and evil in our Creator or Jesus and trinity mathematical calculation.\

when a patient is not well in his biochemistry it is the love of family, in Jesus and God and the holy ghost: that will revive or regenerate the cell even if their is a degree of evil innate in species.[good prevails over evil 100 % of timio deduce: that, in order to make good: satisfy as well being, is by a mathematician.

The former deduction on specie is the first law principle of homo sapiens natures: to argue the god and Jesus Constitution or bile law is[a constant in good nature only: with no bad or evil or war would be what?

example.......Hillary Clinton Barak Obama have a big smile during campaign but in office the must go to war with Isis or Russia look how Pot-in and obama stare one another down and for what! for good? OR .....----_____?

which = two poles of nature in the persons presented in the experiment. one is what? the other is what? it is on the tip of your tou.?

can the student body deduce the the last state of animal is dip-lode or bi polar

can the student body deduce that the gray mass of the giant brain is bi-polar in it nature from and amoeba to the deterioration process it is going thru now as we live in it . + the evidence of our smiles and our frowns of the frontal lobe in which the left brain is the controlled right side and the right brain is controlled by the left side.

p.s.

The complete complexity of specie:

 being [animal- being- good+ evil in nature [LAB.]

Non- human-intelligence of the Animal species:

a. non-development of Nature, Fields of Ccience Science of homo sapiens species.

---^ a Pythagorean perpendicular strait line of intellect being erect or reaching heaven or euphoria or simply Caucasian philosophy of mathematics with calculation being 50 50 but imagine the the the-rum having a souls or souls a third value in calculation process.or 50 50 50 orange red and blue or evident fire. vs a bi polar di plode phenomena of fallacy and psychosis ans also psychotic wars in the bible and in society. of both type of government.= in equal-distance animal nature in the bee in the mosquito in species if derive from God.-----------------------LAW.

---_____ A CURVE AND SPIRALING LINES OF THE FORM OF THE AFRICAN OR PEOPLE OF COLOR.VS, THE STRAIT LINE OR THE ANGLO SAXON...and his ability to think vs. the African ability to break thr infrastructure of the earth physically --------,,< both lesser in the realm of God and the jesus vail or sweet words but yet the anger of his father and the kill of 5000 Scripes

there deduce that the finite nature of mathematics and the eternal nature of mathematics.LAW.

The former is Law and Divinities:

 second ending of manifesto.

Current and frequency of wind and vibration of the is not of a concrete nature but holy ghost of a degree of evil over come by virtues of good in a endless war between the to from beginning to end of time. in molecule and cell as forensic calculation.

The last state of homo sapient is humane is human: one day!

----------------------------------^ heaven = heavens,god + do
gma---< lesser then
is dogma dog in versed for the creator or name nom-dip
lom_____finite + eternity + eternal
_____diploma-
--degree of evil
and lucifer--6
Pythagorean upward equa distances of bi-poles in infinity and eternity=
a constancy of negative dynamical and a absolute non-constant of un-
holy because of the one default of evil of species divine and non divine.

FORENSIC NATURE:

pure eque distance is absolute cleanliness snow white with out blemish
no- dirt on a white TEE shirt non-toxic 100%.perfection no evil at all no-
mistake in calculation of formulas and equations an A NOT a B.

WHITE!

(air) Elohim Son's   qxdratic formula

E,current ray's poly filthy bacteria vs electronic bacteria E,col ray's vs e E, wi is spirit poly vs electronic E, drug's films E , feces hcmc sapiens bacteria E, cocaine alcohol cigarettes false prophet s articles preach er racist

(* aorta) the Son vs. the sun fallacy:}

(leaf with holes put in by birds)

spiraling lines of Spiriticties of color poly numial

~~(~~*~~} current flow dopa-mine frequency

represent the [leaf], p, n, xxxxxxxxxxccience.

wind music. symphonies of silence.

curving lines of whether winds and fumes of bacterium's)Presentation(

MECHANICS Of ALTERNATION OF CURRENTS AND FREQUENCIES

ELOHIM,+{x,polynomial} filth, bacteria - electricity-equal-distance + positive for a bacteria phenomena.

E,{x,p,n color ray's} vs -n, electricity

E,x,p,n,wind spiraling=spirits p,n, vs. {- electricitbacterium,pharrmacy} - color ray's opposite

E,x,p,n,drug films feces of human-vagabondage,pharmacies of major governor presidents ect.-[el,bac,]

E, cocaine ,alcho,- e,b,

e, smoke of cigar cigarettes in the air = - elc,bac.]

E, fallacies s of religion and persos leaders prophets diviners witch

E, Ccience of eyeth + earths poly numial black holes Hippocratic social atmospheres poly numial white and black persos,science and engineering fallacies of non - di plode cell mechanics.

E, x,p,n, + hallucinatory of principalities of the air or - telepathy of Lucifer teams of FARRAKHAN AND THE DISPOSITION OF THE NATION OF ISLAM. AND DEMONSTRATION.

E,xxxxxxxxxxxxx,p,n,] ARTIFICIAL EARTHS WORLDS AND STOLEN OXYGEN FOR THE MAKING OF MAMMON OR MONEY.

ARTICULAR KEY LOPE HOLES ON ELECTRICITY VS. GOD. OR THE PROPER NAMES OF = AN ANESTHESIA.

LAW.

=PERFECTION OF ILLUMINATION IN ITS PURE FORM.

In Stiemeze mathematics on alternations of currents, more electricity need to floe of current's and less stain on the apparatus generating the current flow, vs less bacteria in battery form, less electricity bacteria also less hallucinatory and demonstration , bacteria's more positive telepathy, more telepathic communication less phone and computer apparatus.in Einstein monster of the atomic bomb = Stiemize = absolute demoniac bacteria persos of Ccience.

LAW. BERNARDIAN

p.s phone are starting to explode. why?

the theory of Avance Dortch my father and spiritual guide help me discover the unknown virtue of consolidation of souls ancestor his death and mother. he was illiterate to Anglo Saxon dogma but not to the spirits.

Gandhi was right in plead that the universe need to slow down with the technology things.

PSYCHOLOGY:

I

LUCIFER

L,XXXXXPOLY STAMIZE EINSTIN

L, psychosis psychotic bacteria-ccph}

L,insanity, superabnormaldopamine ph Ccientific pharmacy Anastiga.

IlL,plus triggers ILL, IS HOMO SEXUALITIES MALE FEMALE.

L. ANIMAL CCIENCTICALISM THE SECOND DIMENSION OF CALCULATION ON POSSESSION-ANIMAL-HOMO--SAPIENT EFFECTUATES OF SPECIE.

TWO PERSOS IN DISAGREEMENT OF THE DEMONIAC LOOPHOLE, MAN......!!....... NON HUMAN SPECIE.DEVELOPING MONSTERS POLY NUMIAL, AND MYSELF THE LAST GOOD AND BAD THING LEFT. = THEORIST= THEOTIS DORTCH CALCULATIONIST.

MICHEAL MOODY STIPULATE NEGATIVE SUPER BEINGS OF EVIL = ANOTHER CATACLYSMIC PERPETRATION ANOTHER AMEABA!~ WIND AND VANITIES OF ALL..

NATIONAL GUARD THEOREM CCIENTIFIC-BACTERIUM-REGULATION PHARMACEUTICAL:

persos of me thinks that it is perfect time for the national guard to come forth and create peace in the city of Chicago. the philosophy for this theorem that the police should never be in the state of fear. MC 60.00 as we are; in state of denial.

moon, crime, poly

m,bacterium,criminal minds plus my dark side of schizophrenia being use for good against criminal behavior

m,= non- illumination of Chicago and its business's.

m,=no electricity in the late hours of the night.

m,poly criminal, =electricity regulation. for safety.

m,national guard out in the dark with electricity and flash light.

m, = pure security, appointed guard for a student in task forces, or every student should be appointed a security guard to walk them home from school, church etc.

m, = the reality of gravity before Chicago.

m, apply Rena Descartes theory of effects nature of retaliation and demonstrations of suffer persos or people.

{moon, + Bernadine regulations on crime. looking down from the quadratic formula.

moon, = nocturnal s of quadratic formulas poly nu mail or black folk vs. white folk.

ARTICLE KEY.

 on homo sapient bacterium under a giant MICRO SCOPE

PRINCIPLES OF BACTERIA:

has a political nature of di -plode and parallelisms of Pheroah- Governor Bruce Runner, make slaves work harder in denials of straw. a pure nard senirial.

m, Chicago = mutational state of being, law of eugenics.the dopa mine flow or a celestial motion is same as history Egyptian time of pure evil vs. a pure good or non- illumination of crime cities.

m,p,n =Politca Ccientific'a policia.

LAB FORENSIC NATURE OF BACTERIUM CCIENTIC'A

= A SYMPHONY OF PEACE-FULLNESS

= under the moon.

Amen.

THE DRASOPHELIA FLY AND THE BEE: UNDER MICROSCOPE:

principle 1. flies have a sticky film. color black= the African persos

2. quick to move.

3 understand the homo sapient bacterium.and mentality to try and destroy them. movement super quick.[fly].

4.bi-pole brain of good and evil: an animal in pure nature.

5. THE VIAL AND THE JOGS

dissecting the fly with students , we found that the brain of the fly has a positive effect: fly mucus in a hot jog and a hot vial, effect in their film , is aprior or good for schizophrenia; good because the medicine made of aprior in effect aprior is an adhesive or helps concentration of brain mechanics. in the blood or hematology , muscle, an all coordination,

=LAB THEORY TOO FACTUM.

THE BEE UNDER THE MICROSCOPE:

1. principle:

bee's have a hot chemical in their stinger: in experimentation, poisonous, bi polar like myself or homo sapient. caramel color, opposite the fly , color or black.

2.= positive for fire diet or diet of absorbing the [SON TRINITY} being Elohim and its principles.

3. positive for a quadratic formulas nocturnal being opposite posit? of human Equa-PH'animity far way.vs Eyeth or the hiding of ear]th true form

use ear as a reminder.= LAW OF CIRCLES AND PROPHETCIRCLES

P.S. one must know and understand your far away in contemplation-analysis. around the bend of things.

bee giant

people giant

fly giant the ant a mighty people the bible stipulate.

new moon of Eyeth, SUN OF SON, night time.

= Astro- physics vs. Estro- physically= Heaven KINGDOM OF SPIRITUAL REALM.

eternal realm vs physical realm in beings homo sapient.

WORK SHEET:

THE THIRD ENDING

The AUTHOR:

to whom it my concern: i Bernard C. Dortch suffer much abdominal
pangs from the government and the police: trying to stop me from
practicing my right of freedom of speech. the law or technique that was
use is psycho telekinesis and negative telepathy or hallucination.

my first two books was wrote on two different computer apparatus, both
was hack into: i was scare to death, because i thought i lost my whole life
work, a time it seem as if i was typing with hand cuffs on, also the four
year Barack was in the oval office i felt abdominal pangs.

But, thanks to Eloihem i was taught kung fu by Bruce Lee IN
CHRISTOLOGY, AND MY TWIN THE JEWISH JESUS WAS WITH ME ALL
THE WAY UP TO THE MINUTE. ALSO TUPAC SHUCOR, THE MACHIAVELLI!
AND ME ALSO THE MACHIAVELLI! TO RETURN AGAIN IN MY CIRCLE OF
THINGS.

AMEN.

Physics = the study of natural science and Ccience:

first principle = Atom = an invisible part of nature complex mechanics.

concrete nature. *

<~~~1./~~~2./~~~~~3./~~~~4./~~~~5./~~~~~6.6.6.*~~~~~~~/~~~~/

~~~~~/~~~~/~~~~~/~~~~~~~~/~~~~~~~/~~~~~~~/~~~~=sine~~~~/

~~~~~~~~/~~~~~/~~~~/~~~~~~~/~~~~~~~/~~~~~~~/~~~~~/~~~~

Beast~~~~~~~~~/~~~~/~~~~~/~~~~~~~~/~~~~~~~/~~~~/~~~~/~~~~~/

~~~~Adam+ eve + serpent MAN AND WOMAN + CON ARTIST_____

/_____/_____/_____/_____/_____atoms of earth atmosphere =
deterioration of finite brain or gray mass=deterioration of sine of fallacy
of holy con-artist cepts_____/_____/_____/ university and college +
church-curriculum_____/_____/_____/_____
/_____/_____/_____/_____/_____/__degree of animal
in the perfect -pure calculation of trinity = the number one
IQ.[PQ] if one part of the concept is has guilt it stains the whole
equation.-------/-------/---------/--------/-------/--------/--------
/----------/------/---------/--------/-------/---
---/------/or a speck of dirt on a white tee sh
irt._____Solutionary
state = sine = un-holy + covenant.[atoms and Adams or man =
beast and homo sapeint.but what make the bible satisfy as a positive
= manifesto compilations, written by a man whom name starts with
a B. Bernard dortch and Bernard Shaw.* atoms and the gray mass or
brain functionary states is as a mentally ill patient whom reject the fact
that medicine is for need to adhesive the chemical imbalance of the
brain and if not taken there will be absolute complication of positive
brain functionary state of the brain or gray mass.[deductions of the
fact the time is pure perpetration states because of fallacy of biblical
sine. or illogicality the application of skepticism and the positive field
of mathematical ccience and science. one may deduce cataclysm =
ccience virtue and relapse or death of mentally ill patients= fact of
nature. of natural ccience and science.= perfect and pure psychology
Bernarnian LAW. + the quantum fact that if one put the former nature

in the quantum leap or mechanism of vanishing from one point to a another point in deferential space and time._____/_____/____ _/_____/_____/_____/_____/_____/_____/__/_____/_____/____ _/_____/__Homo Atom'rien Astr'ophenomena's_____ computerized mechanics that send atoms and Adams too the distances of sine + sin.= purgatory or hellish nature and judgment of the long arm of Elohim the trinity or coming in to the secondary enlightenment of another quantum leap of things finite non eternal or eternity which is a realm of heaven non heavens which is a doctors point of view and non dog-------/------- --/----------/---------/--------/--------------/--------/----------/----------- -/--------ma or derogatory etymologies misconceptionalism all thru my father LAW.

LAW AND STATUTE OF QUANTUM PHYSICS ASTRO.

SOLUTION = TWO NATURE'S OF PSYCHOLOGY ON DECEPTIVE ONE A CORRECTIONAL STATE OF A INDUCTIONARYSTATE OF CORPUS BRAIN OF A SCHISZOPHENIA OF CCIENCE AND OF SCIENCE UN DER THE BASE OF MATHEMATICIAN'AL SCIENCES- CCIENCE= BERNARNIAN LAW AND JURY.]

~ absolute infinities, eternities of quantum mechanics)

Millionaire operation article of fire, air and water:

r,b,o,] and ethic:

in the world today the is a grave state of homo sapient bacterium in the parks and political atmosphere polemic of the street ccience idealism of me thinks.

remedy for this negative state of being = huge trucks with a bathing apparatus and showering apparatus for this grave state of the bacteria, coffee and eggs = breakfast for this bacteria of ccience in our cities, truly a cry on to you plead on to the political arena the medicinal committee: this is a ethical crime, and homelessness should be abolished absolutely and shame on the rich for turning the eye to this state of nature.

AMEN.

WORK SHEET:

In may study i discover that there is a haughtiness of concerned and con artist in the eye of modern circumspect of super diabolical personality in the frontal lobe of rappers and scientist whom create tools of mass destruction+ the committee whom award. for almost every nation has tools of mass destruction and for what. to split the atom and take a leap of revelation.

in arrogance and con art persos of my time and history christian a non were persos of war hiding be hind CHRIST JESUS LAY ~~ HANDS CALLING PERSONALITIES GENIUS OVER COMPLIMENTARY FOR THE AVENUE'S OF MAMMON, OVER ENTHUSIASTIC GIVING INTELLECTUAL CREDIT WERE IT IS NOT DO, USE DIABOLICAL PSYCHOLOGY TO GET THREW THE DAZE.= PERPETRATION AND NON PERFECT IDEALISM, ON NATURE OF ORIENT VS. FACTUM OF CCIENCES.. ON RELIGION AND STANDARD CURRICUL'A= OTHINGS AND MORE NOTHINGS:99 VANITY OF THE IMAGINATION, ETYMOLOGY OF NON CALCULATION. A STATE OF PURE CON.

            c.-orange,red,blue formulas,~   ^heavens   ~b.< lesser
figure of speech

                                        ~a.hell, [atom, Adam,= sine.]

(<90 +<99)

SOLUTION OF TRIANGLE: of distance of a, b, c,

(- infinity, - eternity)
(-standard curriculum, - religion)

FORENSIC: LO- EV

(evil = EV, HIDDEN)

(LO=<90 - ANGLE, -360,)

GOOD = NEGATIVE DOCTRINE IN ETYMOLOGY OF DOG --- MA

(-360,- 360,-fire)= (earth, - alpha centurion, poly earth)

Amen.

[cryptography Article key]

THE FINAL END

= STIGMATA.